YOUR ETERNITY

REV. FRANCIS J. REMLER, C.M.

SENSUS FIDELIUM PRESS

Your Eternity: A Heart-to-Heart Chat with Non-Catholics was originally published by the International Catholic Truth Society in 1900, and is in the public domain.

Sensus Fidelium Press edition © 2023.

Print ISBN: 978-1-962639-22-4

SensusFideliumPress.com

CONTENTS

WHAT KEEPS PEOPLE FROM JOINING THE CATHOLIC CHURCH?

PRAYER

INTRODUCTION

All are agreed that it is a grave obligation for a man to give warnings to his fellow men when he knows that serious dangers threaten their property, health or life. To neglect to do so would be highly criminal before God and man. And on the part of those who are thus warned it is but a dictate of ordinary prudence and common sense that they take measures to escape these dangers, no matter how unpleasant or troublesome it may be to do so.

The wireless operator who informed the ill-fated *Titanic* of the danger of collision with icebergs did what he was in conscience obliged to do. And common sense dictated that the officers of that ship should have heeded the friendly warning, even though it meant the loss of the "Blue Ribbon." But they committed the criminal folly of refusing to heed that message of threatening danger; the result was the most frightful disaster in the history of navigation—sixteen hundred human lives lost in the icy waters of the Atlantic, together with the costly ship and its valuable cargo.

We have a parallel in the spiritual world, in the affairs of the soul. Here we find that God has imposed on the priests of His Church the solemn obligation of warning people of the grave and serious dangers that threaten, not their material possessions and their bodily life, but their spiritual goods and their immortal souls. They are in duty bound to point out to men the dangers of eternal perdition, of condemnation to the endless torments of hell. Neglect of this duty renders them guilty of sin.

But if it is a duty for God's ministers to speak words of warning, it is only a dictate of prudence and good sense for people to heed them and take the necessary means of safety. We greatly pity those who are overtaken by some grave disaster suddenly and unexpectedly, but what room is there for pity when men, who have been duly warned, come to grief because they recklessly refuse to take measures of protection? What room is there for pity in the case of persons who are lost eternally, despite the fact that they had been warned?

We have undertaken to write this "heart-to-heart chat" from a motive of sincere love and compassion for our non-Catholic friends. From the Catholic point of view they are living in the appalling danger of exclusion from the Kingdom of God's glory in heaven. It is not always their own fault. Most of them are persons who have been criminally deprived of their rightful inheritance—

the true faith in Jesus Christ. Somewhere back in the line of their ancestry there has been a defection, a giving up of the Catholic religion and the adoption of a false creed. It may have been only in the last generation, it may have been two or three generations ago, or it may have been four centuries ago. Go back far enough, and it will be found that nearly every non-Catholic living today can link up his lineage with ancestors who were children of the Catholic Church. Someone was guilty of the grievous sin of defection from the true faith, and since that day his descendants have been stripped of God's greatest gift to man.

Our sympathy goes out to all our non-Catholic brethren. We know that every one of them possesses an immortal soul that is as precious in the sight of God as is our own. The Precious Blood of the God-Man flowed for them on the Cross. We know that if they are saved, they will exult in the exuberance of heavenly bliss and happiness, in the same way that we ourselves hope to exult; and we know that if they are lost, they will feel for the endless ages of eternity the frightful torments of hell, even as we would feel them, if it should be our misfortune to be lost. These considerations have prompted us to compose this little treatise.

Our aim is to impress on the mind of the non-Catholic reader these three important truths: 1. That the one great and only important work of life is the procuring of eternal salvation, or the winning of the glory of heaven; 2. that salvation cannot be attained except by the fulfilling of the conditions laid down by Jesus Christ, and that no man can presume to choose or lay down his own conditions; and 3. that all non-Catholics who *know* that the Catholic Church is the *only* means of salvation appointed by God, but for any reason whatsoever *refuse* or *neglect* to take steps to join her, and all who at least *suspect* that the Catholic Church is the *only* saving Church, but *neglect* to investigate, are guilty of a *grievous sin against the Holy Ghost,* which exposes them to the danger of eternal punishment just the same as adultery or murder.

In this way is this "chat" meant to be a voice of friendly warning to all non-Catholics of good-will. Our endeavor is to do what we can to save them from the appalling disaster of losing their immortal souls. Accordingly we have tried to speak plainly and without "beating around the bush." Many of the things we have to say will no doubt sound harsh and bitter and perhaps cruel; but that cannot be helped. Many of the things which our Divine Savior said in His sermons hurt His hearers, not only the ordinary people, but also His disciples and apostles. But it was Divine Charity that spoke. He spoke for the good of their souls.

We assure our kind readers that whatever they may find hard or painful in these pages was written entirely in the spirit of earnest solicitude for their eternal welfare. No hurt or offense is in any way intended. Our one aim is to aid them in escaping the most appalling disaster of losing heaven and of being condemned to the endless misery of hell.

May it please God to give His blessing to this

little work that it may be instrumental in guiding very many of our nonCatholic brethren into the one and only haven of salvation—the Catholic Church, and through her into the kingdom of God's glory hereafter.

1

YOUR DESTINY HERE AND HEREAFTER

Let us begin with a few elementary but essential principles.

Have you ever taken sufficient interest in the great subject of your destiny to ask yourself questions like these: "What is the real meaning and purpose of my life? What am I really living for? What is my destiny after death? What will become of me when I die?"

No doubt questions of this nature have often come into your mind and troubled you, sometimes at the most unexpected moments. Even against your will they came and clamored for a hearing and an answer. But you were not in a mood to occupy yourself with them. They were unwelcome intruders in your life of business, or money-making, or study, or the eager pursuit of pleasure and amusement. And so you disregarded them and managed to dismiss them from your mind.

Good common sense, however, demanded that you should have taken time to study into them and find the correct answer. The neglect to do so is a sin against right reason. It is the common source of the loss of heaven. "With desolation is all the land made desolate because there is no one that considers in his heart"—that is, because serious reflection on one's eternal destiny is neglected.

Perhaps you are a member of one of the countless "churches" into which Protestantism has broken up like the stones of a ruined castle, and which persist in continuing to claim the title "Church of Christ." They retain some semblance of religion, but in reality they are only lifeless phantoms of churches. In vain do you seek in them fixed and unchanging definite truth; they have nothing to offer but the shifting sands of purely human opinions. True, they still claim to have the Bible as their guide; but since every non-Catholic is free to interpret its contents to suit himself, we find that there are as many varieties of religion as there are readers of the sacred Book.

Now let me ask: What does *your* church tell you definitely about the supremely important question of your eternal destiny? What does it tell you about sin and its endless punishment in hell? What about the beneficent work of the Redemption by Jesus Christ? What about the necessity of penance and atonement? What about the absolute necessity of God's special help, known as Grace, and of good works, the coin with which heaven must be purchased?

Are you really satisfied that your church is for you the safest means of eternal salvation? Or is it not rather a mere social institution giving you an outlet for various benevolent activities but leaving your heart untouched and your soul empty and hungry? Does it really teach you the true meaning and destiny of your earthly life and offer you the means and helps necessary for attaining the same? Is it not an institution that is more social than religious?

Alas, allow me to say it in all charity—your church is a purely *man-made* creation, a human institution, and as such has nothing divine or Godlike in it. It stands to the true Church of Christ in the very same relation that counterfeit money occupies in regard to genuine currency. As such it has no value before God and no power of salvation. All the founders of our modern churches are counterfeiters in the realm of religion.

Or you happen to be one of the unfortunate victims of our modern system of education without God and religion, which is at the same time penetrated through and through with the crudist form of materialistic evolution. You have been solemnly assured in the name of "Science" that you have not an immortal soul, but that you are merely a higher form of animal, superior, it is true to the horse and the ape, but after all nothing more than an animal; that therefore you have no higher destiny in life than "to eat and drink and be merry, and then cease to be for-ever" when you die, just as happens to the beasts of the field. You have been told times without number that it will be "all over with you" when death comes to claim you. Millions and millions of our people throughout the world have been taught and are being taught this rot, and this they call by the dignified name of *Education.*

All this you may have been taught and thus you may have come to accept as your creed a purely materialistic view of your life and its destiny. But now let me ask you to be honest and sincere. The final issue is so important that you cannot afford to be otherwise. Have there not been moments in your life when you could not be satisfied with the answer which evolution gives to the great question: "What is my real destiny?" Your better nature rebelled against it. It recoiled from it. Destruction and annihilation of your being cannot be the goal. Evolution's answer is cruel, degrading and brutalizing. You are earnestly seeking for an answer that will fully satisfy the yearnings and cravings of the human heart. You want to know the true meaning of your life; you want to be certain what is to be its fate beyond the portals of death.

Despite the boastful vauntings of godless scientists which you may have adopted as your creed, you cannot believe in the utter destruction of your being. It is simply impossible for you to get away from the vexing and disturbing question: "What shall become of me when I die?" It follows you everywhere with the persistency of your shadow, and you cannot feel satisfied with the brutal answer: "All will be over in death." It terrifies you to think of it. You must find an answer that will satisfy you fully.

2

THE TRUE ANSWER

Let us then proceed to give you the true answer. We shall do so by offering you a concise summary of the program of life that has been drawn up for you, as it has been for every man, by God, your Creator and Heavenly Father.

1. You are not of yourself, nor are you the product of blind and purposeless evolution, any more than a watch or microscope is such; but you are a product of God's omnipotent creative power. Infinite love prompted Him to give you your existence, and it is He who is now conserving you every moment of your earthly life. You depend on Him for every breath you draw.

2. Because He is your Creator and you are His creature, He possesses and retains over your entire being a dominion and authority which are absolute in every way. He has unlimited rights over you, which you are bound to respect; but you have no rights of any kind against Him.

3. The marvelous benefits you have received from Him call for gratitude, love and filial service.

You are bound to render Him such a service as He demands of you, not the kind you may find it convenient to choose for yourself.

4. But God does not force you in any way. He leaves you a *free agent*—that is, He does not in the least interfere with your free will. You can choose either to *do,* or *not* to *do,* His will. He uses no force or compulsion of any kind to make you obey or to keep you from disobeying. But while you are free either to obey or disobey, you are not free to escape the consequences of your choice. These you must bear in this life and especially in the next.

5. Strictly speaking, God could have created you with a destiny that is merely *natural,* that is, limited to this earthly life; but He did not do so. He was pleased to assign to you one that is immeasurably high above a purely natural plane. It is called supernatural—that is, above the natural.

6. The principal features of this supernatural destiny are an intimate relationship with God by grace and love, and predestination to the enjoyment of the endless bliss and happiness of heaven. What our divine Savior calls the *kingdom of heaven* is set aside for you as a real and genuine, but entirely gratuitous, inheritance of infinite value.

7. But this inheritance, though a perfectly free and gratuitous gift of God, cannot be obtained by you unless you faithfully fulfill certain well-defined conditions. It partakes of the nature of a reward which must be *earned* or *merited* according to the stipulations made by the donor. Non-compliance means total failure to obtain this inheritance.

8. Your whole earthly life is assigned to you as a period of trial and probation, as a "working day" in which you must work out your eternal salvation. There is no other meaning attached to your life. To win heaven you must "know, love and serve God." If you fail in this duty, you are making a most fatal mistake, the results of which you may have to deplore bitterly throughout the endless ages of eternity.

9. If you have the good sense to keep the thought of heaven always in view and fulfill faithfully the conditions set down for winning it, you can go through life cheered and gladdened by the sweet assurance that endless bliss will one day be your reward exceeding great. God who is true and just and good cannot deceive you.

10. But should you be so foolish as to neglect for any reason whatsoever to fulfill the conditions of salvation, there is no other prospect ahead of you except to be condemned in the next life to be "cast into the hell of fire, into unquenchable flames," where the worm of a reproving and accusing conscience and of bitter remorse shall never die, and where the fire shall not be extinguished for all eternity.

11. Lastly, at the moment of death, your soul will for a time quit the body which was its earthly companion, to receive from the hands of Jesus Christ, its Judge, its proper measure either of reward or of punishment. This the soul will possess alone until the day of the General Resurrection of the dead. On that day your body will be created anew by the almighty power of God, joined once more to your soul as in life, and thenceforth made

to share for all eternity the fruits of your labors on earth—either inconceivable bliss and happiness in heaven or unspeakable torments and misery in the dismal abode of hell.

3

THE SOURCE OF INFORMATION

But you are tempted to ask: "How do you know these things? What is the source of your information?" To this we answer: In His boundless love for man God sent His divine Son into the world to be "the Way, the Truth and the Life" of men. Accordingly Jesus Christ, the God-man, was born into this world, lived among us for thirty-three years, and spent the last few years of His life in teaching us clearly all the things that are necessary for us to know about our supernatural destiny and the ways and means of securely obtaining it.

You can rest fully assured that what He taught is absolutely and infallibly true. His teaching is not like that of men of earthly science or culture. The truths of arithmetic are not more unchanging and unchangeable than are the truths of religion which Jesus Christ taught concerning your soul's salvation. You cannot go astray when you accept them and shape your conduct by His precepts.

But bear well in mind: You must hear and receive these truths with great humility of mind and childlike docility of heart, not with the arrogance of intellectual pride and conceit. The truths of God are not to be subjected to critical tests by human reason as are the teachings of men of science. Christ's verdict stands firm: "He that does not receive the kingdom of heaven as a little child shall not enter into it."

Endeavor therefore to receive God's own instructions on the great subject of your eternal destiny with the necessary dispositions of gratitude, and of humble and childlike obedience. Do not imitate the unhappy Jews of old, who enjoyed the altogether singular privilege of seeing with their eyes, and hearing with their ears the Eternal Son of God-made Man, and witnessed the countless stupendous miracles He worked to confirm His doctrine, but yet remained obstinate in their unbelief. Their greatest grace served only to increase their sin and intensify their punishment. Take heed lest this happen also in your case.

All who refuse to accept Him and all that He teaches are already judged. They are guilty of a grievous sin against the Holy Ghost, which, unless repented of in good time, leads to condemnation in hell just as does the grievous sin of blasphemy, or adultery, or murder. The words of Christ are plain: "He that believeth not is already judged. He that believeth not, shall be condemned." Jesus Christ is therefore your infallible source of information concerning the great question of your eternal destiny.

4

THE OFFICE OF THE CATHOLIC CHURCH

We have shown how Jesus Christ brought the knowledge of eternal salvation into the world. He spent the last three years of His life in instructing men in the most important work that is assigned to them—the saving of their immortal souls by means of the knowledge, love and service of God.

But He was not to remain forever among men. When His task was finished He returned to heaven, and yet the work which He began must go on till the end of time. The truths which He taught must be preserved pure and intact, and must continue to do their blessed work throughout all the centuries down to the last day. The peoples of every climate and race and country are to share in the benefit of His doctrine. All the nations of the entire globe are to profit by the very same truths which the Savior of the world spoke in the hearing of the Jews only. How shall this be done?

God's infinite Wisdom and Power found an easy means. Before leaving this earth, Jesus founded and established what He called His

Church. This He organized with a perfection that is possible to God only, equipped her with all the means she needs for the work she is to do, and gave her the fullest assurance that He Himself would always be with her to the end of time, to guide and direct and fortify her, and give her strength to withstand successfully the ferocious onslaughts of the "gates of hell"—that is, of the world and the devil.

The history of the past 2000 years clearly proves that this Church is the handiwork of God. Diabolical hatred and human malice have left nothing untried to destroy and annihilate her. Inhuman persecutors, cruel tyrants, wily heretics, false teachers, men of unholy ambitions, of intellectual pride, of false science and frenzied hatred of God, have tried in every conceivable way, to destroy and root out this Church and her sacred doctrines, but their efforts have ever been as futile as those of a madman to change the course of the stars or the direction of the wind.

And now we come to a supremely important truth. It is *this Church,* and *no other,* that was established by Jesus Christ for the purpose of teaching the nations of the world the truths necessary for salvation and providing them with the graces which are indispensable to all who desire to reach heaven. Jesus Christ founded this one Church, and no other. There was no need for another. No need for a second one, which would be an improvement on His first attempt. God's first and only Church is perfect and complete. She is not like the works of men. Human institutions, such as societies and governments, are necessarily imperfect and therefore subject to change and improvement, but not so the Catholic Church; she stands firm and immovable and unchanging as the work of the Omnipotent God.

But then we hear so much in our day of the *churches* of the sects. These are almost countless; so numerous and so split up are they that an accurate census of them is impossible, and every one of them pretends and claims to be *God's Church.* Alas, they are blind to the sad fact that every last one of them is a purely *man-made* creation. God had nothing to do with their appearance. And can any sincere seeker after the **Truth** really believe that men like Luther, Calvin, Henry VIII, John Knox, or others, could have received from God the commission either to improve the work of Jesus Christ, or to patch up weaknesses and deficiencies, or even to substitute other means of salvation than those established by the Founder of the Catholic Church?

Lastly, we offer this one thought to our readers for reflection: The rise and appearance of founders of sects and new "churches" is only a proof that the Catholic Church is the Church of Jesus Christ. We see in it only a fulfillment of the predictions which her divine Founder made repeatedly and with which He warned His followers, that His Church would in the course of time be assailed by many false teachers. "There shall arise many false Christs and false prophets and they shall deceive many."—"Many shall go after them."—"Behold, I have told you all things beforehand; go ye not after them."

5

ONLY IN THIS CHURCH IS SALVATION FOUND

God does nothing imperfect, useless or superfluous. When therefore Christ established His Church He meant her to be the one and only ordinary means of salvation for mankind. He instituted no other Church, and gave no man a commission to do so. His Church is all sufficient; all men of good will can find salvation in her, and hence it is that outside the Catholic Church there is no salvation.

Hence all who know of the existence of this Church and her place in God's plan of man's salvation, but for any reason whatsoever refuse or neglect to join her, are a doomed lot. God's mercy, infinite though it is, cannot reach them as long as they persevere in these sentiments. He will not force them to submit, for that would be doing violence to their will; and this God will never do. He leaves every man perfectly free either to enter His Church or keep out of it; to choose life or death, salvation or damnation.

It must be self-evident to every thinking man

that all who seek external life must obtain it by fulfilling exactly all the conditions which God has laid down for this purpose, and not those which the pride of man may choose to dictate. Now one great and indispensable condition of salvation is membership in that Church which Jesus Christ founded for this very purpose.

Men may not like it; their pride may suggest to them all kinds of evasive excuses and pleas for not submitting their intellect and will to her; but there is no helping it if they want to save their souls. By refusing to enter her communion they simply cut themselves off from being sharers in the graces of the Redemption. They are hopelessly (as long as they continue in these dispositions) beyond the chance of salvation. They are committing spiritual suicide.

And why should it not be so? Did not Jesus Christ purchase the chance of salvation for men at the enormous cost of His most Precious Blood shed in unspeakable agony on the Cross? And has He not a perfect right to stipulate precise conditions to those who desire to avail themselves of this priceless grace of the Redemption? Heaven is an entirely free and gratuitous gift. God does not owe it to any man. Man never possessed a right to it. Should we not, therefore, expect that God should have set down very definite conditions, on the fulfillment of which the possession of heaven is made to depend?

The one great condition of salvation is membership in the Catholic Church. There is no other way to heaven but through her. Only in this Church are found the truth and the graces necessary for obtaining life eternal. All other churches are imposters; they are the creations of false Christs and false prophets.

CHRIST MAKES NO CONCESSIONS

There is one striking feature in the life of the Divine Savior that must be noted in connection with our subject. It is His attitude of unbending severity toward the spreaders of religious falsehood and His condemnation of those who obstinately refused to accept the truths He taught. He made no concessions to false teachers. He threatened them with the severest chastisements. The appalling punishment that overwhelmed the lewd cities of Sodom and Gomorrha is declared by Him to be mild in comparison with that which will be inflicted on those who resist His truth. While He showed the most tender compassion to other sinners, He was unsparing and merciless in His strictures on those who were guilty of the spiritual sin of obstinately resisting His heavenly doctrine. No prospect of salvation is held out to these. "You shall die in your sins."

Hear Him rebuke the unbelieving leaders of the Jewish people: "If I tell you the truth, why do you not believe me? He that is of God, heareth the words of God. Therefore you hear them not, because you are not of God. If you believe not that I am He [the Christ], you shall die in your sin."

Again He says: "Woe to you, Corozain; woe to you Bethsaida; for if in Tyre and Sidon had been wrought the miracles that have been wrought in you, they would long ago have done penance in sackcloth and ashes. Amen, I say to you, it shall be more tolerable for Tyre and Sidon in the day of judgment than for you." What a fearful threat is contained in these words!

Surely, the honest and sincere seeker of the truth has all the evidence he needs to convince himself that he must be a member of the Church of Jesus Christ, of the Catholic Church, if he is seriously thinking of attaining his eternal destiny. He must join her, be the cost ever so great. There is no other way in which he can escape eternal misery and win eternal happiness. The insincere and thoughtless are hopeless cases. They are like the unhappy Jews who continued in their unbelief despite the fact that they saw and heard Eternal Truth Itself.

Do you wish to be like them?

WHAT KEEPS PEOPLE FROM JOINING THE CATHOLIC CHURCH?

Having seen in the foregoing section (1) that God has mercifully provided mankind with an effective means of salvation by establishing His (the Catholic) Church; (2) that He meant *this* Church and no other—no man-made Churches— to be the regular means through which men were to be saved; and (3) that Jesus Christ makes no concession to error and falsehood, so that all who willfully refuse to be humble, obedient and faithful members of His Church thereby sign their own sentence of eternal exclusion from heaven, we must now proceed to investigate the various reasons why so many persons hold back and refuse to embrace the Catholic religion, even when they are convinced that this religion is the only divinely appointed means of salvation.

EARLY TRAINING AND ITS RESULTANT BIAS OR PREJUDICE.

No doubt there are vast numbers who keep aloof even to the extent of making no inquiries into the claims of the Catholic Church, simply because their early education was of a nature to ingrain in their minds a disposition to consider her a thing that is essentially evil. It is well known how innumerable calumnies have in the course of time been spread in the world, and continue to live on without any prospect of their ever dying out. They live in books of history and in textbooks used in our schools; they reappear with unfailing regularity in our current papers and magazines; and they form a large part of the so-called religious instruction which the children of non-Catholics receive at school and at home.

Hence it is not surprising that not only thousands but millions from their earliest infancy carry in their minds the conviction that the Catholic Church is a very evil thing; that the Pope is Anti-Christ; that no good can be found where the Catholic religion holds sway. Moreover—we cannot overlook the painful fact—it often happens that the disedifying conduct of careless Catholics contributes its share to the strengthening of this conviction. "These," as St. Paul says, "cause God to be blasphemed."

But what is the position of non-Catholics, who labor under this bias or prejudice against the Church? The answer is not difficult. As long as they are unable to know better and are convinced that their position is the proper one, we can leave them to the infinite mercy of God. If they do not do violence to their conscience and foster deliberate hatred and ill-will against the Church but rather are disposed to learn the truth, we can entertain the hope that sooner or later they will profit by the grace of enlightenment which God will in some way offer to them, and that thus they will become members of the Catholic Church before they die.

But when once this grace has been offered to them and they refuse to make good use of it, refuse to investigate in order to learn the truth, they render themselves guilty of sin—a sin against the Holy Ghost—and thus place themselves in imminent danger of eternal condemnation, just the same as do those who commit sins of the flesh.

HUMAN RESPECT OR THE FEAR OF MEN.

The second reason we shall assign is what goes by the name of *Human Respect or Fear of Men.* The fear of what people will think or say has been responsible for countless acts of omission of good and of countless acts of commission of evil.

This one thought "What will people say?" has ever been the source of immeasurable harm to souls. How many good deeds have been left undone, how many acts of religion neglected, how many otherwise well-disposed persons have been kept from embracing the Catholic religion, simply because the fear of men's adverse and unfriendly and hostile criticism blocked the way! It is really sad and deplorable to see to what an abject slavery this fear will reduce those who in other respects are men of undaunted and even heroic courage! Many who fearlessly face death in a fire or on the field of battle, quail like wretched cowards before the opinions and remarks of the rabble.

This is especially true when there is question of embracing the Catholic religion. What! Enter a

Church which is everywhere so much maligned and despised? A Church that counts among her members such vast hordes of the poorest, the lowliest and most illiterate and ignorant, and of those who have no standing whatsoever in the world? A religion that is sneered at and ridiculed and laughed to scorn by hundreds of the world's most learned men of science and culture?

What! Shall I embrace a religion which emphasizes the supreme importance of spiritual values and takes no notice of material progress, or at least attaches no great importance to it? A religion that insists on duties that are hard to perform, on a long list of commandments that are so repugnant to man's natural inclinations and desire of amusement and gratification of sensual pleasure? A religion which insists on humility, obedience, meekness, chastity and purity?

What would people think of me? What bitter things would my relatives and friends say of me? What adverse criticism would reach my ears from my business associates, employees or employers? What, if the papers got a hold of it and published it for the amusement of all who are ill-disposed toward me?

What! Become a Catholic in the face of all these difficulties? Impossible.

But, dear friend, there is nothing else for you to do, if you are determined to escape hell and win heaven. There is for you no other door through which to enter into life eternal, except the Church of Jesus Christ. Human respect or the fear of what unfavorable things men will say of you must not keep you back. Of what benefit will it be to you to have preserved the good opinion of men by remaining a non-Catholic, when in hell you will forever hear the taunts of the demons reminding you of your consummate folly of having feared men more than God?

No, if you want to be saved, you must not let the fear of human criticism stand in the way. Remember the words of Jesus Christ: "He that shall be ashamed of me and my word before men, of him I will be ashamed before my Father who is in heaven: and he that shall deny me before men, him I also will deny before my Father who is in heaven." And He indicates that the fear of men is a hindrance to the acceptance of His faith, when He asks: "How can you believe, you who receive glory from one another?" Many prefer to forfeit the saving grace of God rather than lose the good opinion of men.

FEAR OF THE ENMITY OF RELATIVES AND FRIENDS.

We have spoken of the fear of men's opinion as an obstacle to embracing the true faith. Let us now consider a more intensified form of this fear—the fear of the enmity engendered in those near and dear to you. That this is a most formidable obstacle is made plain by the repeated utterances of our Divine Savior on this subject. To face the ill-will, hatred and sometimes bitter, unrelenting enmity of those joined to you by the most intimate ties of flesh and blood—father and mother, son and daughter, brother and sister—often means a greater hardship and entails more painful suffering than would imprisonment or torture with the rack.

It will help us much to consider the several passages in which our Lord speaks of this serious obstacle to the embracing of the true religion.

"He that loveth father and mother more than me, is not worthy of me. And he that loveth son and daughter more than me, is not worthy of me." These words are plain and forceful. He that does anything sinful or offensive to God out of love or consideration for his parents, will be adjudged guilty of exclusion from the possession of God. And he who out of love and affection for his children hinders them from doing God's will or induces them to act contrary to their conscience, renders himself guilty of sin and its punishment. We must never do what is sinful out of regard for others, not even our nearest relatives.

Again He says: "If anyone come to me and hate not his father, and mother, and wife, and children, and brothers and sisters, yea, and his own life also, he cannot be my disciple" (Luke xiv, 26). What does this mean? Are we really to commit the sin of *hating* our nearest kindred? No, never. What then does it mean? Simply this, that our love of God must be so great that in comparison with it our love for our relatives will appear to be hatred, just as in the full light of the sun the light of a candle will appear to be darkness. And this proper ordering of love must show itself in that we at no time do anything contrary to the holy will of God, even if by this we incur the displeasure or enmity of father or mother, or son or daughter.

In another place He says: "Do you think that I came to bring peace on the earth? No, I tell you; but I came to bring the sword and separation [that is, estrangement, enmity, persecution]. For there shall be from henceforth five divided in one house; three against two, and two against three. The father shall be divided against the son, and the son against the father, and the mother against the daughter and the daughter against the mother; and the daughter-in-law against her mother-in-law. And a man's enemies shall be they of his own household."

All these declarations of our Lord indicate that the embracing of His faith very often entails the opposition, ill-will, hatred, enmity and not rarely bitter, relentless persecution by those who are nearest and dearest to us by reason of the ties of flesh and blood.

And yet it becomes necessary to brave all this if a person wants to save his soul. To refuse to accept God's grace in His true Church for fear of being cast out from the circle of one's friends and of losing the love and affection of one's parents or children is a grievous sin which entails condemnation to endless sufferings.

Dear Reader, are you one of those who is convinced of the truth of the Catholic Church and of the duty of joining her, but yet hold back from fear of incurring the ill-will and enmity of your loved ones at home? You foresee that you will "bring the sword and separation" into your family; they will be displeased, grieved, angered; they will perhaps disown and disinherit you; they will exile you from the dearest spot you have in this world. What a cruel alternative!

But all things considered, which is the greater evil: to be rejected by your relatives now or by God hereafter; to be condemned to suffer for Christ's sake in this life or to endure eternal misery in the next? Take courage—thousands before you have faced the same difficulty, but they chose wisely.

They gladly incurred the hatred of men in order to secure the love and friendship of God, and they chose to become disinherited exiles from their earthly home in order to inherit the fullness of bliss in their heavenly home beyond the stars.

FEAR OF OTHER SUFFERINGS.

We have not yet done with the question of "suffering for justice' sake." Besides those sufferings, which converts must often endure from their relatives and friends, there are those which are prepared for them, in many ways by the world at large. We have our Divine Lord's assurance that His faithful disciples must be prepared to share His own lot in the world. He makes no attempt at concealing or disguising this hard truth, that fidelity to Him will invite sufferings for them just as naturally as the lightning rod attracts the electricity of the air around it. "If they have persecuted me they will also persecute you; if they have called the master of the house Beelzebub, how much more them that are of his household?"

From the time of our Lord until the end of the world it remains an unchanging truth that Christ's disciples will be subjected to painful sufferings for His sake. His words are plain and admit of only one meaning: "You shall be hated by all men for my name's sake." There were times in the history of the Church when the embracing of the true faith was equivalent to signing one's own death sentence. Thousands, nay millions, have endured the most unheard of and inhuman tortures, and sacrificed their very lives, for no other reason than that they accepted the teachings of Jesus Christ. They are the Martyrs of the Church.

Can you explain this strange state of affairs: Men may join any form of Church they fancy; they may become Anglicans, Lutherans, Calvinists, Unitarians, Mormons, Mohammedans, Buddhists, Christian Scientists, and no one will bother his head about them, but let them become Catholic arid the whole world seems to be leagued against them to make them suffer for their taking this step. Does not this very fact serve as a proof that the Catholic Church is the Church of Jesus Christ, in as much as the predictions of persecution for His sake are fulfilled only in the case of Catholics?

It will pay us to quote a few more of the declarations of our Lord on this point. This is only in keeping with what He Himself prophesied in regard to His apostles and disciples. He made it plain to them that to belong to Him was to be the signal for enmity and persecution: Thus He told them:

"If the world hate you, know that it hath hated me before you. If you had been of the world, the world would love its own; because you are not of the world, but I have chosen you out of the world, therefore the world hateth you. Remember my word that I said to you: The servant is not greater than his Master. If they have persecuted me, they will also persecute you." And they persecuted Him unto the agonizing death on the Cross.

These words are continually being fulfilled. The enmity first directed against Christ in His sacred person continues to be directed against the members of His Mystical Body. Catholics are ridiculed, maligned, calumniated; all kinds of possible and impossible falsehoods are circulated about them and perpetuated in textbooks and works of history and fiction; they are often boycotted in business, in society, in civil and political life; often they are denied a chance to make a living; and every now and then some form of violent persecution by mobs or governments is let loose against them. All this is but what we must expect, since our Lord has foretold it: "You shall be hated by all men for my name's sake. The hour cometh, when whoever killeth you will think that he doth a service to God."

Are you then to face all this danger of persecution? Are you to embrace a faith which the world detests and hates with an undying hatred? Are you to do the foolish thing of exposing yourself, your good name, your reputation, your business, your livelihood, nay, your very life to the danger of ruin and loss?

Yes, if you want to escape the danger of worse sufferings in the next life. "He that shall save his life, shall lose it; but he that shall lose his life for my sake and the Gospel—shall save it." If the fear of persecution and suffering tends to frighten you, then reflect on these words of your future Judge:

"Fear ye not them that can kill the body and are not able to kill the soul; but rather fear Him, who, after He hath killed, hath power to destroy both soul and body into hell."

FEAR OF THE MORAL LAW.

Fear of the moral law deters many from joining the Church.

Most people have more difficulty with the Ten Commandments, especially that of Purity (the sixth Commandment) and that of Justice (the seventh Commandment) than with the entire collection of the Church's doctrines. Often the objection that this or that truth is hard or impossible to accept, merely amounts to casting dust into the eyes of people. The real objection is that certain commandments are hard to observe and there is an unwillingness to live according to the rule of the Gospel.

A missionary had finished explaining the Catholic religion to a group of learned men in India. When he was through they made to him this candid statement: "Father, your religion is very beautiful indeed; we admire it very much. But your morality is too severe; we cannot live up to your commandments." Many objectors to the Christian faith, if they were perfectly honest would not allege difficulty of belief, but difficulty of moral living as the real reason why they refuse to embrace the Catholic religion. It is also the real reason why many Catholics give up their faith.

There is no denying it, it is hard to live a genuinely Christian life. It is no easy task to trample under foot the maxims of the world, and to square one's conduct with the Ten Commandments, the precepts of the Gospel and the maxims of Jesus Christ in one's private, family, social, business, civil and political life. Man's natural inclinations are vitiated by original sin and are strongly inclined toward the sensual pleasures offered by sinful indulgence. The three great lusts—of wealth, of impurity, and of pride—are strong in every man and clamor loudly for gratification. Unless resisted at every point, they become the sources of sins innumerable.

What, for example, is more difficult than to strive to be lowly and humble, and not to foster ambition? What more painful than to resist day in, day out, the strong cravings of one's lower nature for the pleasures of the flesh furnished by violations of the sixth and the ninth commandments? What seems more impossible than the exact fulfillment of the wide commandment of love of neighbor in all its branches, especially that of complete forgiveness of all injuries and that of actual love of enemies! And does not the law of justice in one's dealings with the neighbor often entail many grave hardships, which frighten people from following the dictates of their conscience in the matter of becoming Catholic?

As a matter of common experience, very many non-Catholics imitate the Roman Governor Felix in whose custody St. Paul happened to be. It is related that Felix often sent for Paul and gladly heard him as he explained the doctrine of Jesus Christ. But when Paul spoke of these three subjects: *Justice, Chastity,* and the *Future Judgment,* Felix being terrified, answered: "For this time go thy way; but when I have a convenient time, I will send for thee." As a matter of fact, he took good care that this *convenient* time never came.

This scene is re-enacted countless times. There are many who admire the Catholic faith, are well disposed toward it, know a good deal about it, and are, as a misleading phrase puts it, "Catholics at heart." They know indeed that it is the only faith that can save them, but they find it inconvenient to embrace it, because it would necessitate a change of life and the adoption of maxims of conduct diametrically opposed to what they have hitherto been accustomed to put into practice.

They are not prepared to make this great sacrifice—it costs too much—the surrendering of ill-gotten goods, the forgiving of injuries, the adoption of Christian ideals in marriage, the removal or abandonment of occasions of sin, a life of self-denial and heavenly-mindedness. Rather than submit to the inconveniences and hardships of the Catholic Moral Law they prefer to expose themselves to condemnation to eternal torments hereafter.

Are you, dear Reader, one of them? Then ponder these words of Jesus Christ: "You will not come to me that you may have life: If you believe not you shall die in your sin. He that believeth not, is already condemned."

FEAR OF THE CONFESSIONAL.

Another formidable stumbling block in the way of non-Catholics who may have a desire to join the true Church is the painful ordeal of confessing one's sins to the priests of the Church for the purpose of obtaining their forgiveness and pardon.

What a presumption! What a preposterous demand! Men and women to kneel down before a mortal man like themselves and declare against themselves the most secret sins of their hearts! And this, too, as an indispensable condition of pardon from God! This is downright tyranny of conscience. It is degrading of the dignity of man. Since sin was committed in the sight of God, often unobserved by human witnesses, why should it not suffice for pardon to confess it in the secrecy of the heart, to God directly and alone?

We admit confession is not an easy ordeal. It costs human nature very much. And it would be ever so much easier to confess to God alone than to one of His human ministers. But this does not change matters. It might indeed be otherwise, if *offending man possessed the right to dictate to his of-fended God the terms of pardon;* but as long as *an of-fended God has the full right to dictate terms of pardon to the offending sinner* the above argument loses all semblance of force. It vanishes like the morning mist before the rising sun.

We cannot enter upon a lengthy discussion of the subject of confession. We can only remind the reader, that Our Lord gave the fullness of His own power of forgiving sins to His apostles and their successors, with instructions that they were to use this power for the salvation of those who seriously desire to be saved. There is no question of forcing sinners to repent. Salvation is a matter of the sin-ner's own will. But whoever wants to be saved, must, in case he has committed a grievous sin, ob-tain forgiveness on the terms set down by Him who alone can grant pardon.

We can easily picture how God could have placed much harder conditions for pardon. He might, for example, have obliged the sinner to make a public acknowledgment of his sins, even the most secret and most shameful ones, just as is the case now in auricular confession. In that case, there would be no other choice except to undergo this extremely painful and humiliating ordeal, or go into eternity unpardoned and condemned to the endless torments of hell.

How easy in comparison with this is the ac-knowledgment of one's sins in the secrecy of the confessional to a priest who may be a total stranger to you and you to him; one who is bound by the strictest laws of God and the Church to complete secrecy, and who usually forgets in the course of a few hours the stories of human sin that have been poured into his ears by penitent souls.

And if it still remains a painful task to confess one's sins to a priest, we must not forget, that this very fact is meant to be a part of that penance and atonement which God exacts for our evil deeds. Confession would not be a penance if it were not attended with pain and humiliation.

Persons who have a right understanding of religious things recognize in the Sacrament of Penance one of the most convincing proofs of God's love and mercy toward sinful man. He exacts the very least that still satisfies the claims of His infinite justice when He could have exacted the most rigorous conditions; and He gives to the truly penitent sinner the very same assurance of full and final pardon and reinstatement into His grace and love that our Divine Lord gave to the penitent Magdalen in the banquet hall and to the penitent thief on the Cross.

Some say confession is a human institution. We reply, that if Christ had not ordained it, no Pope and no council could have introduced it. When in 1215 the law was made that every Catholic confess at least once a year it was not that confession was then first introduced, but it was merely defined how often a man must confess if he desires to retain membership in the Church; just as was done in the matter of receiving Holy Communion.

We do not hesitate to say that if confession had not been ordered by Christ but by some Pope, the promulgation of such decree would have estranged more persons from the Church than all the persecutions that have ever been waged in her long history.

Confession is a divine institution, and the divinely appointed means of forgiveness of sin.

THE EXAMPLE OF BAD CATHOLICS.

Finally, there are those who make the bad example set by certain Catholics a pretext for not embracing what they know in their hearts to be the only true and saving faith. This is a very poor excuse, and one that is entirely unworthy of a person of thought and reflection.

Suppose Catholics around you are bad, or even that they were ten times worse than they actually are, would that constitute a good reason why you should rush headlong into eternal perdition? Who is so foolish in times of epidemic contagions to disregard safe rules of health simply because he sees around him persons who pay no attention to them? When men are placed in serious danger of death by some dread disease, like yellow fever or the bubonic plague, they can think of nothing else than how to escape this danger irrespective of what may become of others. They will not hesitate to use heroic means, if necessary. What others choose to do does not bother them. They are concerned about their own personal safety.

Why should you think of acting differently when there is the question of escaping, not a dread disease or a painful death of the body, but the endless torments of the flames of hell? Should you not, out of purely personal motives, employ every means of safety at your disposal, no matter what course others may pursue? Your fate is not in the hands of bad Catholics, nor is theirs in yours. If Catholics lead bad lives and are lost, it is *they* who will suffer, not *you;* if *you* are lost, it is *you* who will bear the penalty of your folly, not *they.*

No, the salvation of your soul is a purely personal affair for you, just as is the maintaining of your health and the saving of your life. And it is only you, and you alone, who can successfully manage this affair. Whether Catholics around are good or bad, does not affect the question of your salvation. If you are saved, it is *you* who will for all eternity rejoice in glory and bless God for His goodness; if you are lost, it is *you* who will for all eternity howl in misery, and curse your inexcusable folly in having made the example of bad Catholics a pretext for your resisting the grace of God.

A FINAL PLEA

Permit me, dear non-Catholic reader, in the spirit of earnest solicitude for your eternal welfare to make a final appeal to you to look well into the question of religion.

As the case stands, you who read these pages, are in one of these three classes of persons: (1) Those who are *convinced* of the truth of the Catholic Church and *know* that only in and through her is salvation possible; (2) those who have *serious doubt* about the truth of their particular church and *suspect* at least that after all the Catholic Church is the only divinely appointed means of salvation; or (3) those who are so indifferent about the affairs of their soul that they pay no attention to them and put aside all thoughts and questions of a religious nature.

If you belong to the class of those who know and are convinced that outside the Catholic Church there is no salvation; or if you belong to the class who feel insecure in their faith and suspect that after all the Catholic faith is the true one —then I must boldly and fearlessly, but in all charity, tell you a truth that will sound bitter and hard, but which is as unchangeable as are the laws of mathematics. It is this:

All those who have received from God the grace to *know* that the Catholic Church is the one divinely appointed means of salvation but for any reason whatsoever refuse or neglect to join her, and all those who have come to doubt the safety of their position and suspect that the Catholic Church is true but refuse or neglect to investigate her claims—are living in the enduring and continuous sin of resisting the Holy Ghost, which is just as criminal in the sight of God—even if not considered so by men—as is the enduring and continuous sin of adultery in a man who lives with another man's lawful wife.

This statement, we well know, sounds bold and harsh. But when carefully examined it will be found to contain nothing exaggerated but merely the naked truth. That this is so, can easily be gathered from the conduct which our Divine Lord manifested toward different kinds of sinners. As we have already seen He was tenderly compassionate toward all classes of sinners except those who resisted His doctrine. He scourged their obstinacy with holy indignation and told them that they could expect no mercy at the hand of God unless they humbled their proud minds and received His doctrine with the humble docility of children.

From this, it is plainly seen that sins against the Holy Ghost, such as that of not receiving the known truth, are greater in the sight of God than are sins of the flesh, and entail more severe punishment.

It is only charity to preach this fearlessly to our non-Catholic brethren; those who are well disposed will receive it gratefully, those who are ill-disposed will have no excuse to offer in the judgment. Whether they like it or not, it is our duty to remind them of the true state of their spiritual condition, and to warn them of the danger of eternal perdition to which they are exposing themselves. We consider it a bounden duty to warn our fellowmen when serious dangers to health and life threaten them; is it not a much more serious duty to warn them of the dangers of exclusion from heaven and condemnation to eternal misery?

As to those who are too indifferent about their eternal destiny to give it serious thought, we can only commend them in charity to the mercy of God by earnest prayer for their timely conversion.

8

A WORD OF ENCOURAGEMENT

When our Divine Savior conversed with His disciples for the last time before His death, He told them emphatically that the world would bitterly hate and persecute them for the one reason that they were His followers. But He also encouraged them to perseverance by reminding them of the reward He had in store for them in His heavenly kingdom. "I will see you again; and your joy shall be full; and no man shall take it from you."

Already in the beginning of His public ministry, in the Sermon on the Mount, He had spoken of this subject, and enlarged on the blessedness of suffering for the sake of justice and virtue and religion. "Blessed are they who suffer persecution for justice' sake, for theirs is the kingdom of heaven. Blessed are ye when men shall revile you, and persecute you, and speak all that is evil against you, untruly, for my sake. *Be glad and rejoice, for your reward is very great in heaven.*"

These consoling words are spoken to all who are in any manner subjected to sufferings at the hands of their fellowmen for the sake of Christ and His faith.

Moreover, all who are afflicted and persecuted by reason of their religion are especially dear to God. God watches over them with a very special providence and assists and sustains them in their trials. He gives them special graces. People sometimes wonder why God does not interfere and remove the sufferings of converts; why He seemingly abandons them and leaves them to the mercy of their enemies; why He allows the powers of evil to harass them and make their life a veritable martyrdom: but they forget that suffering is the price that people must pay for the precious grace of the true faith; and suffering is the tool God employs for preparing souls for occupancy of the higher places of glory in heaven. The saints of God have ever looked upon suffering as an unmistakable token and proof of God's special love for them. As it was with Christ Himself, so it must be with His disciples. "Ought not Christ to have suffered these things, and so to enter into His glory?"

Let us conclude with the argument of St. Peter: "This is thanksworthy, if for conscience toward God a man endure sorrows, suffering wrongfully. For what glory is it, if committing sin, and being chastised for it, you endure suffering? But if doing good you suffer patiently, this is thanksworthy before God. For unto this you are called; because Christ also suffered for us, leaving you an example that you should follow His steps."

Dear reader, our task is done. We plead with you to act wisely and see to the secure attainment of your soul's salvation. God has lovingly placed heaven before you as a destiny, but it must be won by you on the condition of belonging to that one Church which Jesus Christ founded for that very purpose. You cannot look for salvation in churches which are the handiwork of men—of men who for the most were anything but models of virtue and holiness of life. Man-made churches are as powerless to save souls as an artificial acorn is to produce an oak. True, they are more convenient, and appeal more to our sin-tainted nature, because they do not insist on penance and self-denial and confession and other painful practices of religion; they do not call for humility of mind and obedience of will; but for that very reason they have not in them the power to confer the supernatural graces which are essentially necessary for those who are taking the matter of salvation seriously.

An eternity—and endless eternity—of weal or woe of happiness or misery is at stake. Will you not take the safest means to avoid the one and secure the other?

Rest assured, if you accept the grace which God so graciously offers you, and disregard the opinions and persecutions of men, the day of eternity will more than a millionfold repay you for the sacrifices you made to abandon falsehood and accept the saving truth of the one and only Church of Jesus Christ.

PRARYER

Since the acceptance of the true faith is ordinarily
beset with a great many trials and sufferings, special helps are needed by those who desire to obey
the call of grace. These helps will be furnished by
the goodness of God in answer to fervent and per-
severing prayer. Hence those who are seriously
thinking of entering the Catholic Church should
adopt the practice of earnest prayer for light and
strength. For light, that they may come to have a
good understanding of the doctrines of Faith, and
for strength, that they may be able to brave the
difficulties which they must of necessity en-
counter. With prayer all graces can be obtained;
without prayer salvation is impossible even for
the Catholic.

1

AN ACT OF FAITH

O my God, I firmly believe that Thou art one God in three Divine Persons, Father, Son and Holy Ghost; I believe that Thy Divine Son became man and died for our sins, and that He will come to judge the living and the dead. I believe in these and all the truths which the Holy Catholic Church believes and teaches because Thou hast revealed them, who canst neither deceive nor be deceived.

2

AN ACT OF HOPE

O my God, relying on Thy infinite goodness and promises I hope to obtain pardon for my sins, the assistance of Thy grace and life everlasting, through the merits of Jesus Christ, my Lord and Savior.

3

AN ACT OF LOVE

O my God, I love Thee above all things with my whole heart and soul because Thou art all good and deserving of all my love. I love my neighbor as myself for the love of Thee. I forgive all who have injured me and ask pardon of all whom I have injured.

4

AN ACT OF CONTRITION

O my God, I am heartily sorry for having offended Thee, and I detest all of my sins because I dread the loss of heaven and the pains of hell, but most of all because they offend Thee, O my God, who art so good and deserving of all my love. I firmly resolve, with the help of Thy grace, to confess my sins, to do penance and to amend my life. Amen.

www.ingramcontent.com/pod-product-compliance
Lightning Source LLC
Chambersburg PA
CBHW070939120626
46546CB00004B/1479